Before You Leave

A COLLECTION OF POEMS FOR YOU BEFORE YOU LEAVE THE NEST

WRITTEN BY
MELISSA DICKERSON

Before You Leave:
A collection of poems for you before you leave the nest
Is written and designed by
Melissa Dickerson

ISBN: 9798493069109

Dedication

for my child who is preparing to leave the nest

Don’t forget to buy good shoes
They always made you run faster
and jump higher
They ones with the lights
worked best
Splurge on the good pair.

Listen to the wisdom of the trees
They teach us to bend and not break
They teach us that changing
can be a beautiful thing
Embrace their wisdom

Sleep and laughter
are good medicine
for almost anything
that bothers you.

Scatter kindness
wherever you go
The world
needs more
kind words
kind actions
and kind faces
Spread it around

A tree needs roots to stand -
don't forget yours

This world will try to
smother your creativity
Life will get in the way
and you'll push it aside
Don't let it happen
Never stop playing the guitar
Never stop drawing
Never stop writing
Don't let life
smother your creativity
Keep fanning the flames

Never be hungry
don't run the car on empty
and don't be a stranger
You'll always have us
We love you
I hope you enjoy your freedom
I know I did

Forget who they told you to be
Forget who they want you to be
Be you
Be the true, authentic, wild you
Just be you

Sop listening to others
Trust yourself
Trust your intuition
Let your heart
speak louder
than your thoughts
You know how to
handle situations
You know
what to do
Trust yourself

We gave you roots
We gave you wings
Now it is your time
to fly

Slow down
Don't get caught up in
the speed of this world
It's moving too fast
Take the time to
watch more sunsets,
walk in nature,
breathe fresh air,
and soak up the sunshine
Slow down and get outside
Nature heals
It's good for the soul

Start your day with
a good cup of coffee,
positive thoughts,
good vibes,
and love in your heart
Sprinkle it around to others
as you go
through the day

This world will try to harden you
It will try to break your
free spirit
It will try to break the
wild child in you
Don't let that happen
Don't fall for it
Always stay true to yourself
Always keep
your soft heart
and gentle spirit
Cry at sad movies
Read heartfelt poetry
Embrace beautiful song lyrics
Don't let this world change you

Don’t get lost
in this big world
and forget
who you are
Get lost in music,
books, shining eyes,
nature, and
beautiful souls
instead

Let’s sit under
the starry sky
and discuss the
constellations
We’ll talk about
the moon
and the stars, too
I miss those conversations

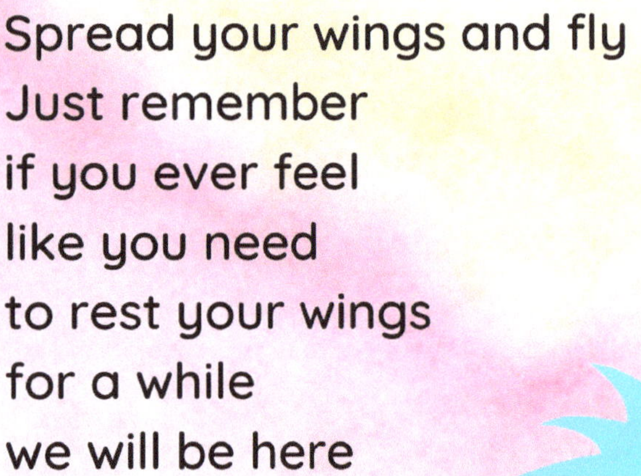

Spread your wings and fly
Just remember
if you ever feel
like you need
to rest your wings
for a while
we will be here

Fly little bird
Fly
We raised you and
had a part
in creating
the brilliant
young adult
you are now
It's time
Spread your wings and fly
You have big work to do
The world is waiting

There are times you'll find yourself
at a fork in the road
There will be a decision
to be made and you
won't know which way to go
Do you go left
Do you go right
Don't make a quick decision
Take as much time as you need
Then, choose the path
that brings you
more positive energy,
more peace,
more calm,
more rest
Choose the path that brings you joy
Don't choose the path other
want you to take
Don't listen to others
Choose your own path
Listen to your heart and
choose your own path

When it feels like your world
is crashing in all around you
and you feel like you can't go on
Remember you are stronger
than you think you are
You are wiser than you realize
You are capable of more
than you know
Remember that

Always be a giver
A giver of love
A giver of strength
A giver of good vibes
A giver of positive thoughts
A giver of good energy

Remember to love yourself
You have a huge heart and
are always giving to others
You are always kind and thoughtful
Don't forget to do the same for yourself

don't fall for the
superficial
bullshit

they'll tell you
you have a pretty face
and a nice body
but that's not important

fall for someone
who tells you
you're a great person
you're smart
you're funny
you're amazing

fall for that shit
not
the
superficial
bullshit

ABOUT THE AUTHOR

Melissa Dickerson is an author, blogger, and creative writer. She has a love of history, family, poetry, and children's books.

Melissa lives in Northeast Ohio with her husband, three grown children, and five grandchildren. She is currently pursuing her creative writing in the form of poetry, fiction, and children's books.

You can find Melissa at www.MDickerson.com and on Instagram at @MelissaDickersonAuthor. Her illustrations and artwork can be found @MDickersonArt on Instagram as well.

www.ingramcontent.com/pod-product-compliance
Lightning Source LLC
LaVergne TN
LVHW071220160826
845679LV00003B/885